T0198979

Therapy for My Soul

Sheena Tomlinson

AuthorHouse™ UK
1663 Liberty Drive
Bloomington, IN 47403 USA
www.authorhouse.co.uk
UK TFN: 0800 0148641 (Toll Free inside the UK)
UK Local: 02036 956322 (+44 20 3695 6322 from outside the UK)

Because of the dynamic nature of the Internet, any web addresses or links contained in this book may have changed since publication and may no longer be valid. The views expressed in this work are solely those of the author and do not necessarily reflect the views of the publisher, and the publisher hereby disclaims any responsibility for them.

Any people depicted in stock imagery provided by Getty Images are models, and such images are being used for illustrative purposes only.
Certain stock imagery © Getty Images.

This book is printed on acid-free paper.

ISBN: 978-1-6655-9022-8 (sc)
ISBN: 978-1-6655-9021-1 (e)

Print information available on the last page.

Published by AuthorHouse 07/12/2021

authorHOUSE®

Contents

Preface

October 2015

Today, out of the blue, I received a call from Author House Publishing and it made me think – I really need to get myself together and turn this dream into a reality as I have procrastinated for far too long in writing my poetry book.

Poetry is my way of expressing myself – mostly when I have been low. I hope that my words resonate with people who have experienced the same things as me and that one day, one of these poems may make history – I am not sure how, maybe turned into a song or just a memorable poem that will be around for years to come creating a legacy to my life on this earth.

"Nothing is easy, but everything is possible"

A little bit about myself

I am an only child of Caribbean heritage. I had the best parents anyone could wish for, although they were quite strict and had old school values, my childhood memories included some of the best moments of my life.

I discovered my talent for writing poetry in my early twenties and later began sharing these with my friends. I realised that this was my way of dealing with my emotions and expressing my thoughts, hence the title 'Therapy for my Soul'.

I had my daughter quite young and she quickly became my driving force.

I started my career as a PA and worked my way up in the Financial Industry. Outside of work I enjoyed travelling to various parts of the world and have to say that I did my fair share of partying!

My life still has and will always have, its fair share of ups and downs. It is how you deal with them I guess, that maketh the man, or woman in my case.

I will get there – as my dad says, "Its long, but it's not forever"

Dedications

To my parents - Without your values, I would not be the woman I am today. You have shown me what a marriage and relationship should be all about - giving, loving, caring and trying. Compromise is what I have seen between the two of you over the years.

I am so privileged to be able to call you my parents. I love you with all my heart and soul.

To my daughter - I know you will make your own mistakes and learn by them. You make me so proud – keep striving for your dreams and never give up. Keep your mind, body and soul, clear always.

To my best friend - Without your patience, understanding and honesty – I am not sure what I would have done at times. From my lowest of lows to my highest of highs, you have been there to encourage and support me through them all. You are one of a kind and extra special!

To my cousin – Thank you for being you and making me laugh so much over the years. You have been instrumental on this publishing journey and I am so very grateful for your support – love you dearly!

May 2021

My father passed away last year. To say I am absolutely devastated would be an understatement.

Dad, may you rest in eternal peace. You are in my thoughts every minute of every day. My entire being misses your presence in this world.

You have given me the determination to get my poetry published.

~ Sheena

2020 Vision

I heard someone say, let's forget 2020
Not me I'm afraid, it's forever etched in my memory
The two metre distance, tested patience, closed stores
No meeting friends or family, just confined to four walls

No getting your hair done, a trim for the men
This is the 'new norm', forget how life was back then
Don't step over the line, wait your turn in the queue
Wait for the orders explaining what you can and cannot do

Not sure how this 'new norm' will truly pan out
"Here comes the big recession!", I hear the Government shout
Things don't look too good, in fact they look bleak
The world got shut down…. For Covid 19 to speak

I often feel fearful, thinking about how this will end
But he said 'Faith' and not 'Fear' would ensure you transcend
From this unprecedented time, which will go down in history – I'm sure
But for now the scientists still search for the inevitable cure

So people of this world, although things, they look grim
Please use this time wisely, during this pandemic we are in
Redefine your values and take the time to reflect
Give this world that we live in, its' undue respect

For so long it seems that we have taken for granted
All the things on this earth, the most high he has planted
Not forgetting loved ones lost, so many have been affected
The impact on lives and economy, mental health – so unexpected

NHS Key Workers risk their lives to save the lives of all others
The lives of our siblings, our fathers and mothers
The new norm? The new lens for this 2020 Vision
Only God can save us from this pandemic related prison

By Enemies Necessary

By enemies necessary
Your words were like a gun to me
You asked me to forgive you, see?
By enemies necessary
Tongue so sharp, heart missed a beat
Actions so vile, could not believe
By enemies necessary
You looked at me like history

By enemies necessary
Rope to my throat, I could not breathe
Evil streak, within your sleeve
By enemies necessary
Haunted me, I could not sleep
Felt you there, beneath the sheets
By enemies necessary
Words in my mouth, but could not speak

By enemies necessary
Hit me hard, knocked to my knees
Stung so bad, venom like the bees
By enemies necessary
Cold blooded mind, about to freeze
Picked those words, so carefully
By enemies necessary
Aim to hurt – your only destiny

By enemies necessary
Like arrow to target, hit perfectly
Just look at what hatred, done to me
By enemies necessary
I sprint, I run – I tried to flee
Felt you there, right next to me
By enemies necessary
Fired those words so eloquently

By enemies necessary
Spit like the venomous snake you be
Those eyes they look, begrudgingly
By enemies necessary
Your being – so filled with jealousy
Revenge is all that you can see
By enemies necessary
Blinded by my pure sincerity - BY ANY MEANS NECESSARY

One Million Lies

One million lies, a million times
A million steps to see a million die
I no longer see a compromise
Lightning Strikes, across dark blue skies
A thief at night – such a cunning spy
Killed the man I know, with one million lies

Couldn't see truth even if you tried
Tears of blood from tightly closed eyes
These damn screams replacing quiet cries
Dark black clouds fill my light blue skies
Release me of these unworthy ties
So many times – tried long goodbyes
Numerous lows, zero highs
Puzzled mind, fails to analyze
Sailing ship – about to capsize

Sunken heart, murdered eyes
Rusted soul, to my demise
Pretty truth, oh those ugly lies
My need for reality, so I can survive
This game you play, without a prize
Holding on to what – is your disguise
Letting go, for me to rise
Experience, has made me wise

Finally! I realized
Finally! I took my own advice
Erase the past, to stay alive
Futile trying to figure out 'Why?'
No story here, have to improvise
- no big surprise
Took a while and countless tries
Was not worth a million sighs
This from me, my last goodbye

To the man I know with one million lies

Unseen

Murdered my hope
Tried to manslaughter my faith
Found me guilty of a crime
Locked me up in these gates
Shackled up my two feet
Handcuffed both my hands
This ain't my life
Didn't build my house in the sand
Prisoner in my own head
Lord, why won't you set me free
I wanna hear those waves crash
Whilst feeling the calmness of the sea

Felt the knife stab me in the back
Blood curdling screams
Is this what it feels like
Nightmares replacing my dreams
They say keep the faith
Don't you ever give in
But I feel myself slipping
My last breath taken in
This wasn't the plan
I ain't committed no sin
It really doesn't matter – this is the here and the now
Just one more breath, then out of this life I shall bow

Hope

I've often sat and wondered
why I'm sitting at this place
You promised not to give me more,
No more than I can take
I could be feeling weak right now,
But all I feel is strong
Refuse to ask 'why me' oh lord
Cos this road – won't be for long

You'll banish all the fear I have
And you will watch over me
You promised if I keep the faith
That you will set me free
I know that in this trying time
All I can do is trust
Never will I give up hope
For me "Hope" is a must
I got this… and with my family
All I feel is blessed
Love will get me through this time
And God will do the rest

Chemistry

Didn't know your name, where you lived,
or how we came to be

You looked so fine, your smell – divine, but oh the
Chem-is-try

When I see you, wow! you touch my world,
And make me feel so proud

Your less is more, the way you walk,
Standing way out from the crowd

When you're in a room, I see only you –
To all others I am blind

Searched the world for you, give you my heart
You are my diamond find

Never will I let you go, with you
is where I'll be

You've got my time, blowing my mind, but
Oh the chem-is-try

When you hold my hand, I'll be the one,
I'll protect you and I'll guide

Making love to you, is what I'll do,
I will always be by your side

You got my soul, you make me whole, my heart-
You hold the key

Never going to let you go, of this I'm sure
You are everything to me

Karma

Karma's coming, oh frenemy of mine
Will give you yours, when you've been unkind
So think again, before it's too late
Karma's the destiny to your never-ending fate!

Don't want to dwell, I wish you well
You were not nice, I paid the price
Under your spell, felt like hell
Bitten once, shy like twice

Beat me down, like I'm the clown
Jokes aside, was on that ride
Kind for weak, no lips to speak
Happy now, you shut me down

Performance great, not gonna hate
Awards to you, none to a fool
Now I'm done, let Karma come
Tables turn, when Karma earns

What goes around, you laugh'n now
Tomorrow's fears, will be your tears
Only then, will you remember when
You start to crack, Karma got you back

Karma's coming, oh frenemy of mine
Will give you yours, when you've been unkind
So think again, before it's too late
Karma the destiny to your never-ending fate!

Single Mother's Perspective

The absent father – present at her birth
You planted the seed, brought life to this earth
But for you, you thought your job was complete
Didn't wait one second to hear her heartbeat

You failed to feed her, whilst I did some chores
Just arguments, raised voices and slammed doors
I can only wonder, the crazy thoughts you had
It's like your brain couldn't compute the importance of the word 'Dad'

Didn't choose any of the schools, or attend not one meeting
Didn't know her favourite colour, nor the friends that she was keeping
I moved house to ensure a better education she had
But where were you then? Where were you?....so called 'Dad'?

Remember her prom, aged just sweet sixteen?
Oh no, you weren't there to see your daughter become a queen
A queen that I RAISED, never bad mouthed you then
Cos I knew she would see – her dad was a coward amongst men

It's ok though, cos she GRADUATED, a 2:1 didn't you know?
She did ok without you, you consistent "no show"
It hurts me so much to witness my daughter in this pain
Pretending she's ok, having to play the damn lying game

I cannot condone this, absent father…. the damage you've done
Remember your life? – You are somebody's son!
You were never there to witness tears falling down her face
Because her father in name only, is an absent disgrace

Not a penny you gave me – towards the baby we created
Just left my baby wondering, if you loved her or hated
Stop the cycle? No, you never stepped up to the plate
Just a bunch of excuses, saying "it's just too damn late"

You were my choice
Regrets - I refuse to have
Cos for my beautiful girl…
I'll be her mum and the dad she never had!

Bereaved

My mind is doing overtime
Can't believe what's taken place
I knew one day, what's happened
Is something I'd have to face

But never did I imagine
That the pain would be this much
The things we take for granted
Like a smell, a laugh, a touch

My soul is torn, spirit forlorn
My heart – broken in two
I know I can, somehow I will
Get through this just for you

You taught me how to be a lady
Stand tall through all the rain
I promise I will show you that
Your teachings were not in vain

I know that you're at peace right now
I know your soul is blessed
So Lord please take good care of him
My father's come home to rest.

Daddy Please Don't Die

Daddy, please don't die
It's too much for me to take
I know that this is selfish
But don't die for goodness sake

Daddy, please don't die
I need to see your face again
I always want to remember 'Now'
Not looking back at 'Then'

Daddy, please don't die
'Cos there's no-one else like you
Daddy, if you leave this world
I'm not sure what I would do

Then suddenly it dawned on me
Then the thought came back again
To leave this world would be ok
If you were not in pain

Daddy if you have to leave
I will treasure the time we had
Just know I love you with all my heart
Rest in Peace my loving dad

Deal, or No Deal

You know that light bulb moment
When it all seems so clear
You just give in to faith
And forget about fear
Positive lines in your mind
Are all that you hear
The place you wanted to reach
Now abundantly near

In the right direction
The only place that you steer
A strong coat of armour
Is all that you wear
That 'I can do' attitude
The only thing you adhere
The path you now tread
Not a worry, nor a care

The dream that you had
Is now finally here
Just laughter, no crying
No more drops of a tear
This is what you were born for
Your hearts own career
No longer blinded by bright lights
See success, so aware

New chapter of your life
No longer see through the rear
Looking straight to the future

Is your dream life from here
Threw away all the burdens
Light is all that you feel
Took this long to get here
From the Court of Appeal

No longer listening to fake talk
Watching actions so real
No longer eating for one
Looking at a champions meal
No longer hurting your feelings
Got the choice of 'no deal'
Didn't know this here feeling
Is what you would feel

Didn't think you could get here
Had to get down and kneel
Prayed to God as your witness
Your despair you concealed
Didn't think you would make it
It was such an ordeal
Things that you went through
Were oh, so surreal

That thing in your life
They call your Achilles heel
Drove away from the negative
Took control of the wheel
So happy in your life
Choose to 'Deal' or 'No deal'

Fight or Flight

Gone from friends to enemies
From holding hands to throwing p's
Went from standing, to on our knees
Conversations, to shouts and screams
We found the I, that's not in team
Replaced the love with being mean
And all because, so it would seem
Making love, should not have been

No longer loving, hating is all
We've gone from floating to freefall
Making one another feel small
There's no story – writing on the wall
Love just made us stand so damn tall
Without the love, we just came to a halt
The good times are over y'all

We should have never – about to recall

Can't bear to be in the same room
No melody in here, just a monotone tune
Fighting's in our blood, bleeding the unknown
The hate we now have – the hostility we've shown
Can't go back to what's past, the seeds are sewn
There's no together here, just me and alone
Childlike actions, question whether we're grown
Leaving my life – for the stars to take me home.

Modern Day

Gone are the days of popping
in and out of shops
To purchase that one item
that you haven't already got
What's my name, my email,
my postal address, my pin?
I just want my item please,
don't want you to know where I'm livin'

It's for points you say,
Points to add to my account
No thanks sir, I just want to purchase,
Pay and then go out
Such attitude, in the air I smell
As I refuse to comply
If I gave you that information
Sir, I'd be tempted to tell a lie

Don't want to give my soul
In order to buy that one thing
Not into the whole spying, the "Big Brother" is watching!
Remember the days when I would pick,
Buy, pay and then just leave
No twenty questions, no bonus points
Or hidden agendas….Please

Abused

A is for the Anger
B is for the Bruise
U is for the way I felt, by that I mean felt Used
S is for the Stench, the alcohol so strong
E is for Every touch, I knew that it was wrong
D is for Death….the amount of times I wished
be it mine, or be it yours – were the words upon my lips
I is for the Image, cannot recall your face
N is for the Noise I stopped – my each and every pace
N is for the Night, those stairs I had to climb
O is for Ostracized; I felt that loads of times
C is for Countless – the things you did to me
E is for Evil, the one you seemed to be
N is for Never, never to let you win
T is for total control, of which I gained within

G is for Guilty, for that is what you are
I is for Isolated, like an isolated star
R is remember – even though I tried to forget
L is longing – longing that we had never met

The letters in this message – one by one I'd like to hurl
Because if you look more carefully, you **ABUSED** an **INNOCENT GIRL**.

Lonely

Lonely don't live here, don't come knocking on my door
Can't take this pain, 'cos lonely got my heartbeat on the floor
I can hear the pounding, but I can't let you in
Please don't bother me, 'cos I'm here with misery
Misery got me crying, tears rolling down my face
When misery has gone, heartache 'gon take his place

Heartache got me burning, in the middle of my chest
When heartache is gone, sleeplessness won't let me rest
Staring at the stars, sparkles looking down at me
Why can't my loneliness be replaced with my happy?
I'm jaded by these feelings, so want a change to come
Say goodbye to unhappy, so happy can take me home

Sometimes I remember happy, but then sadness wonders in
The tears start rolling down my face, then lonely comes back again.

About Time

Just about time that you came and saved me
Just about time when my happiness you gave me
Just about time you put hope through my door
Just about time you picked me up off the floor
Just about time you showered me with success
Just about time you showed me more instead of less
Just about time you gave me faith instead of doubt
Just about time you gave me water in this drought
Just about time I felt rich instead of poor
Just about time I got the key to luck's door
Just about time you stopped me leaning and made me stand
Just about time when you gave me a helping hand
Just about time your shoulder was there for my cry
Just about time – make me want to live instead of die.

Soldier

I'm a fighter, I'm a soldier,
never give up on my dreams
I'll go to war, I done told you,
my nice persona ain't what it seems
Go to battle, fight my cause,
I will see my name in lights
Got my armour, got my ammo,
I sure ain't afraid to fight

Standing firm now, see my target
Bout to blow up all these walls
They try to hurt me, knock me over
But I ain't the one who falls
You tried to slay me, take my soul away
But this fight is mine to win
Not giving up now, I'm still standing
To lose this battle is a sin

I gave my all now, see you fall now
Body knocked down to the floor
Won't be beaten, or defeated,
I'm a soldier to the core
Getting praises, it's amazing
Don't give up on what is yours
Fight for your dreams, know what I mean
I got my own rules and my laws

Hot Summer

As I sit upon this tube and off to work I go
You came and sat right next to me
But there's something you should know

The smell that wafts right past my nose,
Is really not the one
A mix of stilton and stale milk
Wrapped up in gone-off bun

Sorry to have to say this,
But it really has to go
Has neither friend, nor family
Told you, you have B.O?

Please hold a fresh and use 'Right Guard'
Before leaving your abode
Or please, to choose some other seat
If you do not know the code

To leave your house and smell like that
It really is a sin
The smell is like you took your clothes
And washed them in the bin

Once clean and fresh, you'll really see
What life has to hold
No longer will you look uncouth
And smell like days old mould

With sun and heat about to hit
Within a day or two
I much prefer the 'Lynx' effect
Than that awful smell of 'YOU'

Poverty

Ain't it a shame, all this blame
and the pain that we're living in
Don't wanna try, say goodbye,
give up on life, cos they're giving in
Paying bills, have no frills,
some have debt that they're swimming in
All they want is to breathe,
take a breath and to live again

See them cry, want to die
Cos they're tired of the struggling
They work so hard
No ace card
Just the joker coming back again
Shuffled pack, lost the knack
The deck of life, they can't seem to win
Instead of up, they go down
Round and round and then come back again

Heartache and pain, just the same
These two are just the norm to them
"get up and go" left long ago
With 'hope' and 'believing in'
It's sad to see, what will be
They don't care and cannot see the end
They lost all hope, can't even cope
For themselves, they can no longer fend

Do they sink, do they swim
Stay afloat, or stop achieving things
Lost their voice, lost their choice
And the air that they were breathing in
So when we're down, smiles a frown
Take a moment to reflect within
To the rest, we are blessed
Remember Life is a blessing sent

Friend of Mine

When we were young and foolish
We never imagined life could do this
Rip out your sanity, tear it limb from limb
Life made you drown, cos you could not swim
Your mind – not your own, such an unfortunate thing
To witness the mess that you are now in

Where did you start losing the game we can't win
When did your fight for life become just a whim
The feeling of numbness is where you begin
Not really aware that your soul you're killing
Pumped so full of drugs that you're no longer feeling
They say to "expect the worst", your prospects are thin

This isn't life, not the way you're living
Groundhog day takes on a new meaning
Can't focus on the bills, the work, or the beating
Wondering if things are gonna change, begging, praying, God willing

Things can only get better, that's not what you're hearing
All you know is your sanity - which the thief is now stealing
Angels, please help her – the hurt she's concealing
Bring her back to her youth and the good things she was dreaming.

Love to Hate

Oh thin line between love and hate
Fingers to a fist extend to my face
Is this another argument, or just a debate?
My destiny seems far – in the closeness of my fate
Thin line between reality – and what to me is real fake
Doesn't give a damn about anyone – all about the take
Doesn't know how to hold, just to shove or to shake
Are you an enemy, or supposed soul-mate?
Love the beat of a heart? No you long for it to ache
Want that "special" bond, only to make it break
Rocking me to sleep, so you can 'shout' me awake
Loving my style just to make me look a state
Your egos on time, but your self-less-ness is late
Wings of an angel, with the bite of a snake
Lips gentle as a feather, words a tonne of weight
Lost in this madness – an open and shut case
Act with less speed and a touch more haste
It's called the thin line between love and hate

The master of a game – one player to be found
Picking me up, so you can knock me down
Encouraging a smile, so you can make me frown

Knowing Me, Knowing You

Are you the one who laid your head, down on my thighs?
Looking up to the midnight skies
Whilst I listened to your problems, praying for God to solve them?

Sad, but every bit true – I know me, but I don't know you

Are you the one who shared - your each and every care?
Whilst I gently massaged you down,
just to take away your frown?

Sad, but every bit true – I know me, but I don't know you

Are you the one who slept, whilst I lay beside you and wept?
Listening to your breath,
wondering what we had left

Sad, but every bit true – I know me, but I don't know you

Are you the one who's free and decided to erase me?
From the corners of your mind,
memories are all I can find

Sad, but every bit true – I know me, but I don't know you

Are you the one whose actions, shout louder than your words
It's ok cos I heard them
and now I choose to burn them

Sad, but every bit true – I know me, but I don't know you

Am I the one who cried, when your actions said goodbye
Self-absorbed and so consumed, my heart your home, now alone

Sad, but every bit true – I know me, but I REALLY DIDN'T KNOW YOU!

Layers

I see beneath your layers
I'm not as fickle as you
I know behind the façade
Is your personality – number two
Trying to hide the real person
Fooling no-one but yourself
Because some years down the line
The lies – fell off the shelf

Pretending to be what you're not
Gemini behind closed doors
Putting on your Dr Jekyll suit
Leaving Mr Hyde there on the floor
But you forgot you have to wear him
To go meet with insincerity
I realized though, when I saw you
It was personality number three

How can there be such deceit
Will you ever grow up and stand tall?
You beat me so hard, I was hurting
Had to pick my years up off the floor
What was it in those words of yours?
Oh shit – personality number four
Word sprinkled with hurt and hate
Intention – cut to the core

Don't you know your pretty
But your ugly is underneath
Don't you know your pretty
Is hidden by your deceit
Don't you know your pretty
Can't seem to wander in
Because your so called pretty
Never really has ever been.

Not Broken

Don't try to fix me, because I am not broken
Don't say my words, when I have not spoken
My eyes wide shut, heart closed – no longer open
Don't try to control me, I'm not your token

My tears still falling because of the pain you've awoken
I've given up trying – forgot all about hoping
No laughter, no love, this feeling is not a joke, and
I'm done with the heartache, my spirit you've broken

I try to hide the hurt, jaded, tired – unspoken
Please put the pieces back, make this puzzle unbroken
Lord knows I've tried, but it just isn't working
Like Rhi Rhi said "Take a bow" close the curtain

My heart doesn't lie, I know this for certain
I'm tired is all, you to me an aversion
Done being the one to carry this burden
Release me from this load – take away all the hurting

Man Up

This could have ended so amicably
But you wanna come and try to take the p*** out of me
So now you're going to see that 'bitch' side of me
"I am a man of my word" that's what you said to me
"Don't worry about it ", he said "I got your money"
6 months down the line you want to try and play me
Well listen to me now and listen carefully
I don't take things light, I take them literally
So if you say you're gonna do it, I expect it to be

Ignoring my text, my calls when you knew it was me
Too damn weak to have a grown conversation you see
The man I met is gone, treated me gracefully
Replaced him with someone else whose just a kid, around 3
Trying to treat me wrong – disrespectfully
True colours you've shown, it's just my back you will see
This situation could be handled so differently
But a point you want prove, you are nothing to me

Take your dollars, I got mine – I'm ok you will see
Worked hard, so damn hard for this position I'm in
You can't get 'one up' no 'one upmanship' on me
Cos I'm not that ghetto chick you done slept with and leave
Take your pram and your toys and your immaturity
Cos I'm done with this bull, I just had to leave
As crazy as this is – I know it is not for me
When you see the man around, that you used to be
Tell him I said 'hi' but as for you, you to me are ……HISTORY

Delusional

He said:

Did you really think I meant it
You should have looked into my eyes
When I told you that I cared for you
It was just a tonne of lies
When I kissed you it meant nothing
You were zero in my life
Did you believe me when I told you I
Wanted you to be my wife?

Did you really think I meant it
You should have read the signs
Although my book seemed genuine
You should have read between the lines
I made you think I loved you –
That you meant the world to me
But it was just about my ego
That meant everything, you see

Did you really think I meant it
When I said you were the one?
If that was what I yearned for
You would have met my son
Just enough rope that I gave
My own version of lies truth
No need for explanations,
Didn't need to show the proof

Did you really think I meant it
When our bodies intertwined?
I didn't mean that either -----
That was lies, upon more lies
You should have been much stronger
Then maybe you would see
You and me together,
Would never ever be

She said:

That's ok because I got it
I'll never change myself for you
Cos someone's out there somewhere
Whose truth will be their truth
He will not lie, nor deceive me
He'll love me and be done
You think that I believed your lies?
Think again……'**Delusional**' one

Black Man Type of Love

Your flow is so different
Skin glistening, it's magnificent
Though they try to knock you down – try to
Make you insignificant
But to us, you are brilliant
Making moves, just so militant
Don't let them tell you any different

We love you irrespectively
You keep loving us unconditionally
We love you back so effortlessly
Your determination especially
Along with such tenacity
The heart beats most significantly
Witnessing your growth – so prolifically

Consider this my summary
WE LOVE YOU UNEQUIVOCALLY